A Guide for U

S0-BBY-369

The Best Christmas Pageant Ever

in the Classroom

Based on the novel written by Barbara Robinson

This guide written by Laurie Swinwood

Teacher Created Materials, Inc.
6421 Industry Way
Westminster, CA 92683
www.teachercreated.com
©1994 Teacher Created Materials, Inc.
Reprinted, 2000
Made in U.S.A.
ISBN 1-55734-437-X

Illustrated by
Blanca Apodaca

Cover Art by
Wendy Cipolla Boccuzzi

The classroom teacher may reproduce copies of materials in this book for classroom use only. The reproduction of any part for an entire school or school system is strictly prohibited. No part of this publication may be transmitted, stored, or recorded in any form without written permission from the publisher.

Table of Contents

Introduction

A good book can touch our lives like a good friend. Within its pages are words and characters that can inspire us to achieve our highest ideals. We can turn to it for companionship, recreation, comfort, and guidance. It can also give us a cherished story to hold in our hearts forever.

In *Literature Units*, great care has been taken to select books that are sure to become good friends!

Teachers who use this unit will find the following features to supplement their own valuable ideas.

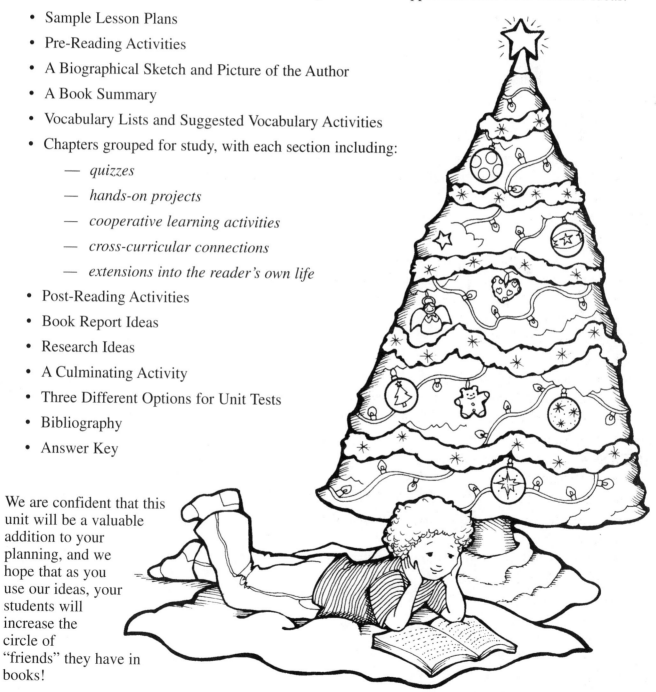

- Sample Lesson Plans
- Pre-Reading Activities
- A Biographical Sketch and Picture of the Author
- A Book Summary
- Vocabulary Lists and Suggested Vocabulary Activities
- Chapters grouped for study, with each section including:
    — *quizzes*
    — *hands-on projects*
    — *cooperative learning activities*
    — *cross-curricular connections*
    — *extensions into the reader's own life*
- Post-Reading Activities
- Book Report Ideas
- Research Ideas
- A Culminating Activity
- Three Different Options for Unit Tests
- Bibliography
- Answer Key

We are confident that this unit will be a valuable addition to your planning, and we hope that as you use our ideas, your students will increase the circle of "friends" they have in books!

Sample Lesson Plans

LESSON 1

❖ Introduce and complete some or all of the pre-reading activities found on page 5.

❖ Read "About the Author" with your students. (page 6)

❖ Read the book summary with your students. (page 7)

❖ Introduce the vocabulary list for Section I. (page 8)

LESSON 2

❖ Read chapter 1. As you read, place the vocabulary words in the context of the story and discuss their meanings.

❖ Choose a vocabulary activity. (page 9)

❖ Create life-size characters. (page 11)

❖ Compile a Christmas Recipe Book. (page 12)

❖ Write holiday poetry. (page 13)

❖ Begin reader's response journals. (page 14)

❖ Administer the Section I quiz. (page 10)

❖ Introduce the vocabulary list for Section II. (page 8)

LESSON 3

❖ Read chapter 2. Place the vocabulary words in context and discuss their meanings.

❖ Choose a vocabulary activity. (page 9)

❖ Create a reindeer ornament. (page 16)

❖ Bake and decorate sugar cookies. (page 17)

❖ Research customs around the world. (page 18)

❖ Create a photo essay. (page 19)

❖ Administer the Section II quiz. (page 15)

❖ Introduce the vocabulary list for Section III. (page 8)

LESSON 4

❖ Read chapter 3. Place the vocabulary words in context and discuss their meanings.

❖ Choose a vocabulary activity. (page 9)

❖ Create felt puppets of the Herdmans. (pages 42 and 43))

❖ Design an angel. (page 21)

❖ Discuss how to deal with controversy. (page 24)

❖ Write a thank-you letter for being given a chance. (page 25)

❖ Administer the Section III quiz. (page 20)

❖ Introduce the vocabulary list for Section IV. (page 8)

LESSON 5

❖ Read chapters 4 and 5. Place the vocabulary words in context and discuss their meanings.

❖ Pick a vocabulary activity. (page 9)

❖ Choose a Herdman. (page 27)

❖ Design dioramas of the pageant. (page 28)

❖ Create a picture-book version of the story. (page 35)

❖ Write about the "Herdmans" in your life. (page 30)

❖ Administer the Section IV quiz. (page 26)

❖ Introduce the vocabulary list for Section V. (page 8)

LESSON 6

❖ Read chapters 6 and 7. Place the vocabulary words in context and discuss their meanings.

❖ Choose a vocabulary activity. (page 9)

❖ Make gingerbread houses. (page 32)

❖ Write a script for a puppet show. (page 33)

❖ Present your Picture Book. (page 35)

❖ Write a letter to Barbara Robinson. (page 36)

❖ Administer the Section V quiz. (page 31)

❖ Introduce the vocabulary list for Section VI. (page 8)

LESSON 7

❖ Discuss any questions that your students may have about the story. (page 37)

❖ Assign book report and research projects. (pages 38 and 39)

❖ Begin work on culminating activities. (pages 40-41)

LESSON 8

❖ Administer unit tests 1, 2, and/or 3. (pages 44, 45, and 46)

❖ Discuss the test answers and responses.

❖ Discuss the students' opinions and enjoyment of the book.

❖ Provide a list of related reading for the students. (page 47)

LESSON 9

❖ Celebrate with the culminating activities.

Before the Book

Before you begin reading *The Best Christmas Pageant Ever,* it will be helpful for your students to have some background information on the author and story. Here are some activities that may work well in your class.

1. Predict what the story might be about just by hearing the title.

2. Predict what the story might be about just by looking at the cover illustration.

3. Discuss other books by Barbara Robinson that students may have heard about or read.

4. Discuss fiction vs. non-fiction.

5. Create a bulletin board for the book. Display other books by Barbara Robinson in the reading corner.

6. Read aloud one of her other books to your students.

7. Share biographical information about the author with your students.

8. Share the Christmas story with your class.

9. Answer the following questions.

   - Have you ever:

     — been in a Christmas pageant?

     — known a child who was thought to be the "worst kid in town"?

     — learned a valuable lesson?

     — thought about the true meaning of Christmas, or any other special holiday?

10. Write descriptions of what makes a child good or bad. Share your ideas with your class.

About the Author

The Best Christmas Pageant Ever
by
Barbara Robinson

Barbara Robinson was born in Portsmouth, Ohio on October 24, 1927. When she was in fourth grade, she began writing as a hobby, for fun. She received her B.A. degree from Allegheny College in Meadville, Pennsylvania in 1948. Before her marriage to John Robinson, in 1949, she worked as a librarian. Today, she lives in Berwyn, Pennsylvania with her husband. She has two grown daughters.

Mrs. Robinson is the author of fifty short stories, which have appeared in magazines like *McCall's, Ladies' Home Journal,* and *Redbook.* She is also the author of five children's books, *Across From Indian Shore* (1962), *Trace Through the Forest* (1967), *The Fattest Bear in the First Grade* (1969), *The Best Christmas Pageant Ever* (1972), and *Temporary Times, Temporary Places* (1982).

"Each book that I have written for boys and girls is also a book I have written for myself," Mrs. Robinson says. "If I don't find the story exciting or interesting or funny, if I don't enjoy the characters or care what happens to them, I don't think boys and girls will either." She especially enjoys writing about the adventures of America's past, and also enjoys doing the research for that type of book. She doesn't outline her books, which for her is an advantage. "Since I don't plan my books in outline form," Mrs. Robinson explains, "I am often in the position of the reader, asking, 'What's going to happen next?'"

Mrs. Robinson has written both a play and a film script for *The Best Christmas Pageant Ever.* In 1983, it was made into a movie for ABC. She has won the Georgia Children's Book Award, Young Hoosier Award, and was named Pennsylvania's Writer of the Year for *The Best Christmas Pageant Ever.* She has just finished another book about the Herdmans which will be published later this year, and she is currently working on an early American adventure story for young adults.

The Best Christmas Pageant Ever
by Barbara Robinson
(Harper Keypoint, 1972)
(Available in Canada, UK, and AUS: HarperCollins)

The Herdmans are, without a doubt, the worst kids that ever lived. They burn down buildings, smoke cigars, and grow pussy willows in their ears. They are the biggest bullies in the school, using blackmail and bruises to get their way. But none of the six Herdmans ever, ever get kept back in a grade. Even though Claude Herdman didn't know his ABC's nor his colors, shapes, or numbers, he still passed first grade. If he didn't pass, Miss Brandel would have had both Claude and Ollie Herdman together in her class, and no teacher was crazy enough to let herself in for two Herdmans at once.

It all begins when Mrs. Armstrong breaks her leg. Mother takes over the Christmas pageant, but she never dreams that before she is through, the whole town will be upset with her. The Herdmans are suddenly very interested in church, having been told they can find plenty of dessert there.

Before long, they bully their way into being the main cast for the pageant. They call the Wise Men a bunch of spies, Imogene (as Mary) is ready to clobber anyone who comes near her baby, Jesus, and the shepherds shake in fear whenever the Angel of the Lord (Gladys) comes near. The town is in an uproar over the whole situation. Everyone shows up for the pageant just to see what havoc the Herdmans will wreak.

But the biggest surprise of all comes from the Herdmans themselves. They had never heard the Christmas story before this year, yet their interpretation truly makes it the "best Christmas pageant ever."

Vocabulary Lists

On this page are vocabulary lists for each section of the book. Vocabulary activity ideas can be found on page 9.

SECTION I
(Chapter 1):

cussed	blackmail
clonked	horrified
double-jointed	collared
contagious	bobcat
volunteer	hysterical
hydrangea	penitentiary

SECTION II
(Chapter 2):

pageant	intermediate
pot-luck	congregation
primary	hymns
tradition	contribution
slouching	coordinator
rehearsals	manger
shepherd	sentiment
privet hedge	collection basket

SECTION III
(Chapter 3):

pews	ridiculous
volunteer	sacrilegious
sprouted	barge
insane	minister
circumstances	pussy-willow
sympathize	rowdy

SECTION IV
(Chapters 4 and 5):

outlaws	trough
snitching	myrrh
espoused	stable
swaddling	retire
frankincense	honor
disgraceful	sly
squinched	antenna
communion	bureau
saloon	vengeance
ornaments	ancestor
truant	villain

SECTION V
(Chapters 6 and 7):

audience	admire
parsonage	refugees
uproar	crooks
pitched	confer
colic	snuffed
bath-salts	congregation
poinsettia	dress rehearsal
choir	milling
ice pick	spotlight
whirled	cockeyed

Vocabulary Activity Ideas

On the preceding page, there are vocabulary words listed for each section. You may wish to divide your class into teams. The teams may find the words in the context of the book, define them, and each team member may record the words and their meanings in a vocabulary notebook.

The Best Christmas Pageant Ever is rich with vocabulary. Use the additional ideas below to help your students learn and retain some of that vocabulary.

❑ Have your students create a **Picture Dictionary** of the words. Design a cover, have it laminated, and bind the finished work. Display it in a prominent place in the room. Donate it to the library at the end of the year.

❑ Challenge your students to a **Vocabulary Bee.** This is similar to a spelling bee, but in addition to spelling each word correctly, the students must also correctly define each word.

❑ Play **Vocabulary Mum Ball.** One student throws a ball to another student, saying one of the vocabulary words before throwing. The student who catches the ball must define the word to stay in the game. If the student can't define the word, or drops the ball, he/she is out of the game.

❑ Using old game boards, play **Vocabulary Champ.** One student is the vocabulary master. The "master" has cards with the vocabulary words on one side and their meaning on the other. Each student must be able to give the correct definition of the word on the master's card in order to roll the dice to move. The "champ" is the first person to reach the end of the game board.

❑ Play **Vocabulary Charades,** where the words are acted out and teammates guess the correct answer.

❑ Encourage your students to **use the vocabulary words in their own writing each day.** Have them "dazzle" their friends and family by using the words in their spoken language as well.

❑ Play **Team Definition.** Group your students into teams. Give each student a slate and a piece of chalk. Give the whole class one of the words to define. Each member must write the definition on his or her slate. If everyone on the team has the correct answer, the team earns a point. (The teacher keeps score on the blackboard.) The team with the most points, at the end of a given period of time, is the winning team. This game may be varied. The teacher might give the meaning and the team members give the word, or the team may be requested to give the word and the correct part of speech, or they may be asked to write the word in a sentence.

Most likely, you have many more ideas to add to this list. Try out your ideas. See if experiencing vocabulary on a personal level increases your students' vocabulary interest and retention.

Quiz Time!

1. On the back of this paper, tell who the Herdmans are and write a descriptive paragraph about them.

2. How did the Herdmans burn down Fred Shoemaker's toolhouse?

   _____

   _____

3. The firemen didn't get any doughnuts. What happened to them?

   _____

   _____

4. Describe the Herdman's cat. Illustrate it on the back of this page.

   _____

   _____

5. Claude brought the Herdman's cat to school. Tell what happened.

   _____

   _____

6. How did Imogene blackmail her classmates? _____

   _____

7. Where is Mr. Herdman?_____

   _____

8. Who takes care of the Herdmans? _____

   _____

9. Who is the author of this book? What is the copyright date?

   _____

   _____

10. Why didn't Mrs. Herdman want to stay home with her children?

   _____

   _____

Create Life-Size Characters

Barbara Robinson does a terrific job of describing the characters' actions in *The Best Christmas Pageant Ever*. Her descriptions make it easy to picture Imogene sneaking around to blackmail her classmates or Gladys whopping any child who gets in her way. In this activity, students will blend the book descriptions with their own imaginations and create life-size characters.

Materials:

- One large roll of white newsprint
- 5" x 8" (13 x 20 cm) cards
- tempera paints
- paintbrushes

Directions:

- Divide class into teams of three or four students. Tear or cut the newsprint into 6' (180 cm) sheets of paper, and provide each team with seven of the sheets. Then, using the descriptions given in the book of Imogene, Leroy, Claude, Ralph, Ollie, Gladys, and Mother, have the teams draw life-size characters of each. Also have them paint their characters, using the tempera paints.

- Then direct each team to paint a background scene of a pageant setting on the white newsprint. Mount the characters on the background painting.

- Direct the teams to write a descriptive paragraph for each character on a 5" x 8" (13 x 20 cm) card. The cards can be glued next to the characters they describe.

Note to the Teacher:

- You may wish to display the characters and their descriptions on a classroom wall, in the hallway, or in the library.

Christmas/Holiday Recipe Book

Christmas time always seems to evoke memories of special foods—cookies, candies, breads, etc. Your students, no doubt, also associate special recipes with thoughts of Christmas or other holidays. Encourage your students to share these special recipes, and create a Christmas/Holiday Recipe Book.

Materials:

- Two sheets of manila tagboard
- Colorful construction paper (one sheet per student)
- Festive recipe cards (one per student)
- Rings (for binding)
- Crayons, rulers, markers

Directions:

1. Have students bring in a copy of their favorite Christmas recipe or special holiday recipe from home.

2. Have each student copy the recipe onto the festive recipe card. Glue onto a sheet of the colorful construction paper.

3. Use two additional sheets of construction paper for a front and back cover; decorate the cover and bind all recipes into a holiday cookbook.

4. With the manila tagboard, create a library card and pocket. Glue the pocket on the back cover, and place the library card in the pocket. Allow your students to sign the book out. Stress to your students that experimentation with the recipes at home should always involve supervision and family helpers.

Note to the Teacher:

As an option to the single copy of the Christmas/Holiday recipe book, consider making copies of the recipes for each student. Have students decorate their own covers and take their books home. As a part of your Christmas celebration, you may wish to choose several recipes from the cookbook to make with your students.

Personal Poetry

Imogene's perception of the Christmas story is intensely personal, so personal she ended up crying and walking into the furniture. Choose any holiday that you feel especially strong about, and write a poem. A cinquain is an interesting form of poetry. Follow the outline below to create a Christmas or holiday cinquain of your own.

Line 1 - Noun (2 syllables)

Line 2 - Adjectives (two)

Line 3 - "ing" describers (three)

Line 4 - A sentence or phrase

Line 5 - Synonym of Line 1

An Example:
Christmas
Joyous, magical
Waiting, wondering, unwrapping
A time for family gatherings
Holiday

Now select your own special holiday. Find words to describe it on the lines below, and create a cinquain of your own.

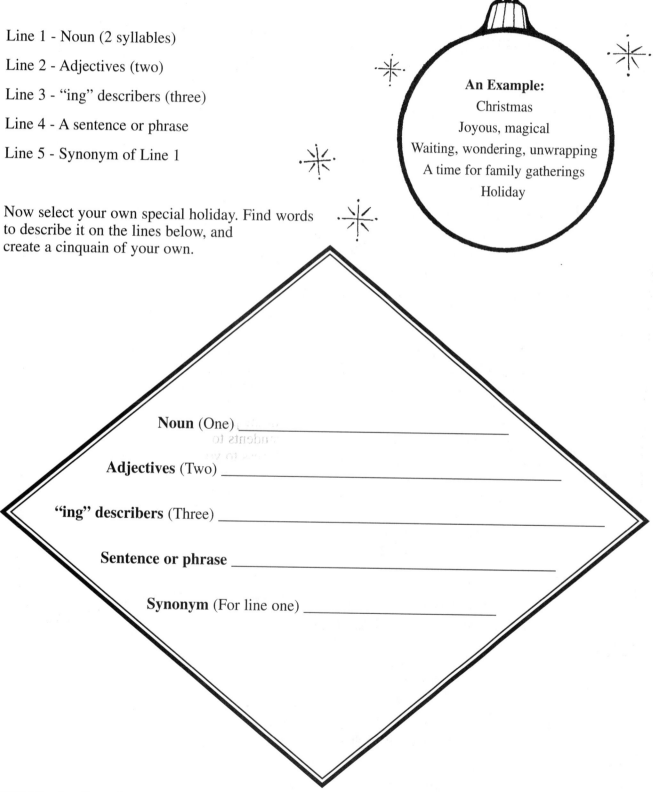

Noun (One) _____

Adjectives (Two) _____

"ing" describers (Three) _____

Sentence or phrase _____

Synonym (For line one) _____

Reader's Response Journals

One reason avid readers are drawn to literature is because of what it does for them on a personal level. They are intrigued with how it triggers their imaginations, what it makes them ponder, and how it makes them see themselves. To enable your students to have this experience, incorporate Reader's Response Journals in your plans. In these journals, students can be encouraged to respond to the story in a number of ways. Here are a few ideas.

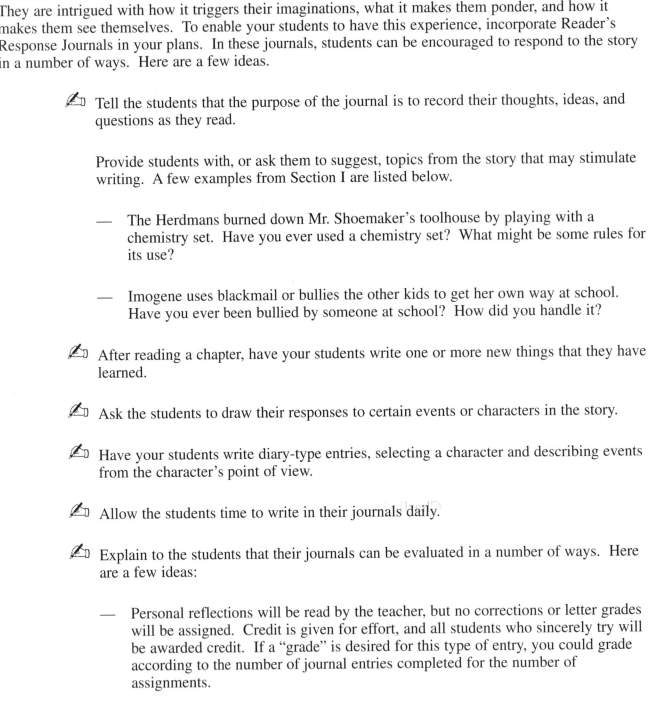

✍ Tell the students that the purpose of the journal is to record their thoughts, ideas, and questions as they read.

Provide students with, or ask them to suggest, topics from the story that may stimulate writing. A few examples from Section I are listed below.

— The Herdmans burned down Mr. Shoemaker's toolhouse by playing with a chemistry set. Have you ever used a chemistry set? What might be some rules for its use?

— Imogene uses blackmail or bullies the other kids to get her own way at school. Have you ever been bullied by someone at school? How did you handle it?

✍ After reading a chapter, have your students write one or more new things that they have learned.

✍ Ask the students to draw their responses to certain events or characters in the story.

✍ Have your students write diary-type entries, selecting a character and describing events from the character's point of view.

✍ Allow the students time to write in their journals daily.

✍ Explain to the students that their journals can be evaluated in a number of ways. Here are a few ideas:

— Personal reflections will be read by the teacher, but no corrections or letter grades will be assigned. Credit is given for effort, and all students who sincerely try will be awarded credit. If a "grade" is desired for this type of entry, you could grade according to the number of journal entries completed for the number of assignments.

— Non-judgmental teacher responses should be made as you read the journals to let the students know that you are reading and enjoying their journals.

— If you would like to grade something for form and content, ask the students to select one of their entries and "polish it."

Quiz Time!

1. What is a Christmas pageant?

   _____

   _____

2. What part does Charlie play every year?

   _____

3. What is Mother's usual contribution to the pageant?

   _____

   _____

4. Who is usually responsible for the performance?

   _____

5. Why does Mother end up doing the pageant?

   _____

   _____

6. What does Charlie like best about Sunday school?

   _____

   _____

7. Who was always giving Charlie bruises?

   _____

8. Why is it Charlie's fault that the Herdman's came to church?

   _____

   _____

9. Why did the Herdmans come to church?

   _____

   _____

10. What did Imogene do when the collection basket was passed in front of her?

    _____

    _____

Reindeer Ornaments

It has long been a Christmas tradition to decorate Christmas trees with homemade ornaments. Create the reindeer ornament below for your Christmas tree in an effort to make this your "Best Christmas Ever." (If you don't celebrate Christmas, make the ornament for a friend who does or simply as a winter decoration for your home.)

Materials:

- Two clothespins
- Glue
- Felt (red, green)
- Small glue-on eyes (may be purchased in any craft store)
- Ribbon (red or green)
- Scissors
- Glitter

Directions:

1. Place one clothespin right side up, and the other upside down. Place the top of one beside the top of the other, and glue together. (One clothespin forms the body of the reindeer and the other clothespin forms the antlers.)

2. Apply a small dab of glue to each eye and attach to the reindeer's face.

3. Cut two small pieces of felt. Decorate with glitter. Glue one to the front of the reindeer, and one to the back.

4. Cut a piece of ribbon, eight inches (20 cm) long. Tie the ends together. Attach to the reindeer by looping and tying it around its neck. Hang from the remaining ribbon.

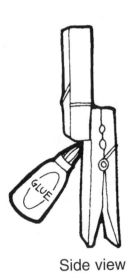

Side view

Front view

Sugar-Cookie Treats

Another Christmas tradition that many Americans follow is the baking and decorating of sugar cookies. All children enjoy cookies (Leroy Herdman visited the church because of the promise of dessert), so even if some students don't celebrate Christmas, they'll enjoy the baking and decorating and eating!

Ingredients:

- ½ c. (118 mL) shortening
- 1 c. (236mL) sugar
- 1 egg
- 2 c. (472 mL) flour
- ½ tsp. (2.5 mL) soda
- ½ tsp. (2.5 mL) salt
- ½ c. (118 mL) sour milk
- 1 tsp. (5 mL) vanilla

Materials:

- Mixer
- Two bowls
- Two cookie sheets
- Cookie cutters
- Rolling pin

Directions:

1. Cream sugar and shortening together. Beat in egg.
2. Sift flour, soda and salt. Stir alternately with sour milk.
3. Combine all ingredients, mix well.
4. Roll out half of mixture on a floured surface. Flour cookie cutters and cut out cookies. Place on a greased cookie sheet. Bake at 400° degrees F (200° C) for 12 - 15 minutes.

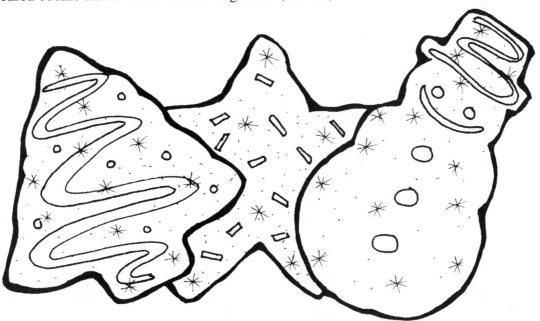

Christmas Customs Around the World

Each country celebrates Christmas with its own traditions, recipes, and folklore. For example, in our country, it is traditional to decorate a Christmas tree and place gifts beneath it. We celebrate Christmas with special gingerbread and sugar cookie recipes, some handed down from generation to generation. Our folklore celebrates elves who help Santa at the North Pole in making and delivering gifts to good girls and boys all over the world on Christmas Eve.

These customs differ from country to country. First, share your own ways of celebrating Christmas with the rest of the students in your class. Your family tradition may involve celebrating Hanukkah or some other holiday. Then, check out the reference section in your library, and choose a country to explore. Use the table below to write the facts, as you find them, about your country's Christmas celebration. Finally, share this information with your class in an oral report.

Country: _____

Folklore: _____

_____

_____

_____

Customs: _____

_____

_____

_____

Traditional Foods: _____

_____

_____

_____

Picture This!

Not everyone celebrates Christmas. Even those who do celebrate Christmas have their own traditions that make their celebrations unique. Using the information students obtained from researching various countries' customs, create a photo essay that demonstrates a variety of celebrations.

If you don't have a camera, ask if you can borrow one from a parent. Divide the class into teams of three or four students. Have each team decide which country's customs to role play (make sure the teams choose different countries). The teams should brainstorm, then list which customs they'd like represented in photos. Each team should choose a specified number of customs, perhaps four or five. Provide additional time for the teams to discuss how they should role play each custom so it will photograph well. Encourage them to bring in props or clothing to make the pictures appear real. You can even supply art materials so they can create backdrops or props.

Then take pictures of the teams depicting the holiday customs of their chosen country. Have plenty of film on hand, so you can get two or three shots of each custom (you want to ensure that enough pictures turn out). Have the film developed, hand the teams their pictures, and have each team create a photo essay.

Materials:

- Photos
- 12" x 24" (30 x 61 cm) tagboard (for each team)
- Markers, crayons
- Masking tape
- Stencils

Directions:

1. Stencil the name of your country and its special holiday at the top of your piece of tagboard.
2. Roll masking tape on the back of each photo and mount them on your tagboard.
3. Stencil a caption below each photo to explain what it represents.
4. Illustrate a border and decorate around the photos.
5. Share your team's photo essay with the rest of the class.

Note to the Teacher:

You may wish to display the photo essays by hangings them from a clothesline in your classroom.

Quiz Time!

1. One lady was always calling Mother about the pageant. What was her name?

   _____

2. Alice Wendleken always had the same part in the pageant. What was it?

   _____

   _____

3. Who was standing at the door when Mother was on the phone?

   _____

4. What was Father's biggest complaint about Mother's involvement in the pageant?

   _____

   _____

5. Who volunteered to be Mary?

   _____

6. What part did Elmer Hopkins always have in the pageant?

   _____

   _____

7. Who wanted to be Joseph this time?

   _____

8. Why didn't anyone else volunteer for any of the parts in the pageant?

   _____

   _____

9. What caused Ollie Herdman's earache?

   _____

10. How did the community react to the fact that the Herdmans were going to be the cast in the pageant?

   _____

   _____

   _____

Angelic Creations

The casting of a Christmas pageant always includes angels. In *The Best Christmas Pageant Ever,* all the primary kids were angels, a number of others were in the angel choir, and Gladys Herdman was the Angel of the Lord. Many people top their Christmas tree with an angel and use angels in their holiday decorations. Following the directions below, create an angel for yourself or to give as a gift.

Materials:

- 1 clothespin (wooden, without a spring)
- tissue paper (one 16" x 24"/ 41 x 61 cm sheet per angel)
- 1 pipe cleaner
- yarn (hair) (One 12" / 30 cm piece per angel)
- 1 rubber band
- white glue
- scissors
- gold paper twist
- pattern pieces below

Directions:

1. Fold the tissue paper in half. Lay the skirt pattern piece on folded tissue paper. Pin in place and cut five pieces.
2. Lay the pattern piece for the wing on a piece of tissue paper. Pin in place and cut one.
3. Lay the pattern piece for the dress top on a piece of folded tissue paper. Pin in place and cut two.
4. Lay the pipe cleaner on the long edge of one of the dress top pieces. Glue in place. Wrap the pipe cleaner in the tissue paper, by rolling it to the other end. Fold in half. Glue to the back of the clothespin. Bring around to the front to make the angel's arms.
5. Cut the other dress top piece in half, lengthwise. Fold in half (lengthwise). Lay one piece from back to front over one shoulder, and do the same on the other shoulder, so that both pieces cross in the front and the back. This forms the upper part of the dress. Glue in place.
6. Turn the clothespin upside down. Attach the five skirt pieces by overlapping them around the "waist" of the angel, upside down. Wrap the rubber band around the top of the skirt pieces, to hold them in place. Pull the pieces down, one at a time, toward the angel's "feet," forming the folds of the dress.
7. Fold the wing piece along the fold line. Glue in place.
8. Cut strips of yarn and glue to top for hair.
9. Make a circle with the gold twist. Glue in place as the halo.
10. Fold the hands (ends of the covered pipe cleaner) and glue in place.

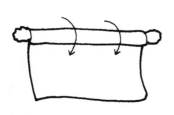 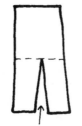  

Angel Pattern

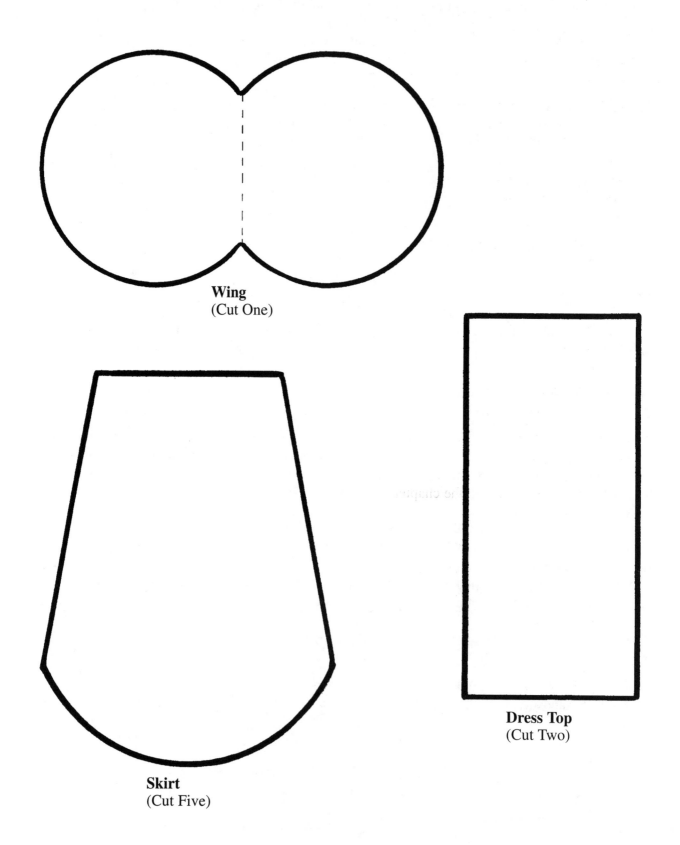

Wing
(Cut One)

Skirt
(Cut Five)

Dress Top
(Cut Two)

Read, Think, Illustrate, and Present

Students often gain a richer understanding of a story if they are given the chance to think about and illustrate it. Divide your class into groups of four. Have each team sit in a circle; then choose one member of each team to be the facilitator.

Facilitator: The facilitator will read the first four pages of chapter three; each member will take turns reading four pages, moving around the circle in a clockwise direction.

Timer: The person on the facilitator's left will be the timer. The timer will allow enough time for the reading, and twenty minutes to create the illustrations. (You may vary times to the needs of your class.)

Materials:

- Multiple copies of *The Best Christmas Pageant Ever* (one per student)
- Markers and crayons
- Large (8" x 12"/ 20 x 30 cm) white construction paper (one for each student)

Directions:

1. Take turns reading chapter three, as explained above.
2. Create an illustration for the section of the chapter that the team members read, numbering the bottom of the paper with a 1, 2, 3, or 4, showing the part of the chapter they read (the first, second, third, or fourth part).
3. Share team illustrations with the whole class.

Note to the Teacher:

If your class doesn't divide evenly by four, you can step in to take over one of the readings, or have a couple of students double up on the readings (they can then choose which section to illustrate). You may wish to have the children display their illustrations around the classroom. Have the class discuss their various interpretations of the chapter.

Nothing Like a Controversy!

When Mother is given the job of directing the Christmas pageant, she realizes it is a much harder task than being put in charge of the pot-luck supper, but she has no idea how difficult it will prove to be. She finds herself in the middle of a major controversy. "Controversy" means a conflict of opinion. How would you deal with the situation? In groups of four, answer the questions below. All members of the group must be in agreement before an answer is recorded. Share your answers with the whole class, and discuss.

Questions:

1. What does Mrs. Armstrong mean when she says, "There are no small parts, only small characters?"

   _____

   _____

2. If you were Mother, how would you handle Mrs. Armstrong?

   _____

   _____

3. In your opinion, should the Herdmans be allowed to be in the pageant? Tell why.

   _____

   _____

4. What did Reverend Hopkins mean when he reminded everyone that Jesus said, "Suffer the little children to come unto me," and Jesus meant all the children, even the Herdmans?

   _____

   _____

Writer's Challenge:

Pretend that you are Mother, and write a letter to Mrs. Armstrong. Tell her how you feel about doing the pageant, her many phone calls, and the Herdmans.

Ever Been Given a Chance?

Mother gives Imogene a chance to be all that she can be when few others would have given her that opportunity. Close your eyes and visualize a time in your life when someone made a difference for you by giving you a chance. Maybe it was a friend, a parent, a teacher, or a relative.

On the lines below, write a note to that person, telling him/her about your experience, what it meant to you, and thanking him/her for giving you that chance. Mail your note or give it directly to the person. If you can't think of anyone who gave you a chance, write a note to your teacher describing future chances you would like to be given.

Quiz Time!

1. What was the "Herdman smile" like?

   _____

   _____

2. What did Gladys and Ollie do to the primary Bible?

   _____

   _____

3. Where did Gladys sleep when she was born?

   _____

   _____

4. How did the Herdmans react to the Christmas story?

   _____

   _____

5. How did the Herdmans feel about King Herod?

   _____

   _____

6. Where did the Herdmans go the next day to learn more about Herod and Jesus?

   _____

7. Who was Kind Herod?

   _____

8. Why was Alice keeping notes on the Herdmans' behavior?

   _____

9. In the beginning, many mothers offered their babies to play the part of baby Jesus in the pageant. Why did they change their minds?

   _____

   _____

10. What did Mother decide to use for Jesus in the pageant?

    _____

Choose a Herdman

Have you ever looked at something from another person's point of view? In this activity, you'll get to do that. You'll choose one of the Herdmans, explain his/her viewpoint of the Christmas story, and then illustrate him/her.

Materials:

- Large, white construction paper (12" x 14"/ 30 x 36 cm)
- Tempera paint   • Glue
- Fabric scraps   • Scissors
- Yarn   • Buttons

Directions:

1. Choose one of the Herdmans (Gladys, Ralph, Imogene, Claude, Ollie, or Leroy).
2. Fold your paper in half. On the bottom half, pretend you are that Herdman child, and write a journal entry which tells the Christmas story from your chosen Herdman's point of view.
3. On the top half of the paper, illustrate whichever Herdman you are (paint the face, etc.) Cut the scraps of fabric for clothing and glue in place. Add yarn for hair and buttons for eyes.

On the lines below, describe why you chose the Herdman you did.

I chose _____ Herdman because _____

_____

_____

_____

_____

_____

_____

_____

_____

_____

Note to the Teacher:

You may wish to have the children share their work and discuss their interpretations with the entire class. Display their work in the classroom or in the library.

Dramatic Dioramas

One creative way to depict a scene involves constructing a diorama. Its three-dimensional effect often intrigues students. In teams of four, create a dramatic diorama of the pageant.

Materials:

- Shoeboxes
- Paste
- Yarn
- Oaktag
- Tempera Paint
- Fabric scraps
- Scissors
- Construction paper

Directions:

1. Place the shoebox on its side, lengthwise. Using construction paper and paint, design the background scene on the inside walls of the shoebox. Create a manger with the oaktag.
2. Cut figures for the characters from the oaktag, decorate with the yarn and fabric pieces, and place in the diorama.
3. If you'd like, include the Star of Bethlehem and the Angel of the Lord in the background.

Note to Teacher:

You may wish to display the dioramas in your classroom or in the library.

Plant a Christmas Tree

The pine tree has long been the traditional Christmas tree in America. Using the directions below, plant a pine tree in your classroom. When the tree is large enough, help our environment by planting it outside.

Materials:

- Small pine tree
- One large pot
- Pebbles (enough to cover the bottom of the pot)
- Potting soil (enough to fill the pot)
- Gardening trowel

Directions:

1. Fill the bottom of the pot with the pebbles and one quarter of the potting soil.
2. Place the tree in the pot.
3. Fill the rest of the pot with the soil, packing it loosely around the base of the tree.
4. Keep the soil moist, but not soggy. Fertilize monthly, spring to fall.
5. Place in diffused sunlight most of the year, but in direct sunlight during the winter months.
6. Minimum temperature should not exceed 50 to 55 degrees.

Extension:

Find out how new pine trees begin to grow.

The "Herdmans" in My Life

Barbara Robinson has created a definite image for us in her description of the Herdmans, from Imogene stealing from the church collection basket to the pussy willow that grows in Ollie's ear. We have known children who were considered the class "bullies" or who were wild and behaved like the Herdmans. On the lines below describe the "Herdmans" in your life. Tell about your experiences with them. Use vivid description in creating them as Barbara Robinson has done with the Herdmans.

Note to the Teacher:

You may wish to compile your students' stories into a book about the "Herdmans" in their lives. Print copies for everyone in the class.

The Herdmans in My Life

by

_____

_____

_____

_____

_____

_____

_____

_____

_____

_____

_____

Use the back of this page if you need extra room to write.

Quiz Time!

1. Who was using the church the night of dress rehearsal?

   _____

2. What did Alice put on her eyelids to make her look more lovely?

   _____

   _____

3. Imogene's ears had been pierced. Did a doctor do it for her?

   _____

4. What was Imogene doing in the lady's room?

   _____

   _____

5. Why was the fire department called?

   _____

   _____

6. What happened to the applesauce cake?

   _____

   _____

7. How were the Herdmans like the real Holy Family?

   _____

   _____

8. What did the Wise Men bring as their gifts?

   _____

   _____

9. How did the Herdmans improve the pageant?

   _____

10. Why was Imogene crying?

   _____

   _____

Design Gingerbread Houses

It has long been a Christmas tradition in this country to create gingerbread houses as a part of the festivities of the holiday. The directions below will allow you to create a more simplified version of the traditional gingerbread house by using graham crackers in place of the gingerbread. Work on your own or with a partner. Use your imagination and have fun!

Materials:

- Graham crackers (5 whole crackers per house; each cracker has 4 sections)
- White frosting ($^3/_4$ cup/177 mL per house)
- Oaktag (8" x 12"/ 20 x 30 cm)
- Christmas candy
- Tin foil

Directions:

1. Cover the oaktag with the tin foil.
2. Heavily frost the bottom edge, lengthwise, of two graham crackers. Place on the oaktag, upright and resting on the frosted edge. These will be the two sides of your house.
3. Break one graham cracker in half along the middle line of the cracker, forming the front and back of your house. Frost the bottom and side edges and stand in place.
4. Frost the top edges of your house and place two more graham crackers so that their outer edges meet as the peak of the roof. Frost the peak and the roof. Add candies for decoration.
5. Display your gingerbread houses in the classroom or in the library.

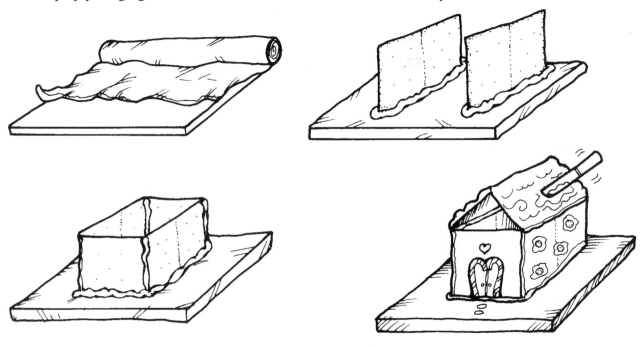

Puppet Script

In teams of four, decide which section of the book you would like to present as a puppet show for younger children. Brainstorm your ideas below. Decide on the main ideas to be presented and write the script that will best represent your ideas. Be sure to include a narrator.

Brainstorm:

List all of the parts of the book that your group would enjoy doing. Then narrow it to one choice.

Main Ideas:

List all of the main ideas that need to be presented in your puppet show.

Characters:

List all of the characters that you will need.

Puppet Script *(cont.)*

Using the format below, write your puppet script. On the line provided, write the name of the character that is speaking. In the parentheses, add any stage directions, such as "speaking softly" or "raising his hands in anger." Then, after the colon, write what your character is saying. Refer to your copy of *The Best Christmas Pageant Ever* for accuracy. Use the back of this page if you need more room.

Narrator: _____

_____

_____

_____(   ): _____

_____

_____

_____

_____(   ): _____

_____

_____

_____

_____(   ): _____

_____

_____

_____(   ): _____

_____

_____

_____

Present Your Picture Book

In this activity, students will not only illustrate main scenes from *The Best Christmas Pageant Ever*, but they'll also have the chance to create sound effects that enhance their illustrations.

Materials:

- Heavy white paper, 14" x 18"/ 36 x 46 cm (20 pages)
- Manila tag, 14" x 18"/ 36 x 46 cm (for cover and back of book)
- Tape recorder and/or video camera
- Hole punch
- Metal rings
- Main ideas typed on strips of manila tag

Directions:

1. Paste the strips of main ideas onto the heavy white paper.
2. Divide students into groups of four. Give each group two pages from the book.
3. Have each group illustrate their pages.
4. Have group practice presenting their illustrations with sound effects. (See below.) Record the story and sound effects on tape.
5. Have students rehearse presenting their illustrations with the tape recording. Have students show each illustration in pairs.
6. Videotape their presentation.
7. Invite friends and family in and share their video.
8. Compile the pages into a book with a child-designed cover, and bind with rings.

Sound Effects:

- ✦ Rub a wooden spoon across the face of a grater.

- ✦ Fill glasses with different amounts of water. Tap gently with a spoon.

- ✦ Stomp feet or clap hands on a tabletop to simulate footsteps.

- ✦ Play a favorite tape, or use a keyboard and play your own music in the background.

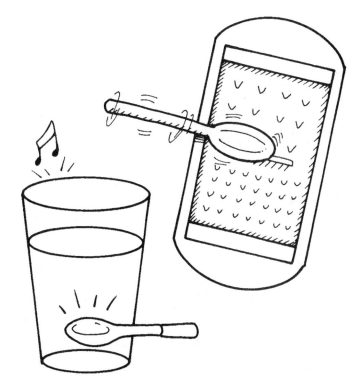

Write to Barbara Robinson

Often the best response that writers can receive to their writing is to hear from their readers — you!

On the lines below, write a letter to Mrs. Robinson.

Include any questions that you may have about the Herdmans or about Mrs. Robinson. Illustrate your favorite characters and enclose them with your letter. Be sure to include your return address so that Mrs. Robinson may write back to you. Send your letters to: Mrs. Barbara Robinson, c/o Avon Books, 1790 Broadway, New York, New York 10019.

Dear Mrs. Robinson,

Note to the Teacher:

You may wish to have your students write their rough drafts on this page. After they have proofread and edited this copy, they may write their final copy on teacher or student-created stationery.

Any Questions?

When you finished reading *The Best Christmas Pageant Ever*, did you have some questions that were left unanswered? Write some of your questions below.

_____

_____

_____

_____

Work in groups or by yourself to prepare possible answers for some or all of the questions you have asked above, and those written below. When you have finished your predictions, share your ideas with the class.

- Why did Mr. Herdman leave his family?
- Would the children have behaved differently if he hadn't left?
- Where is Mr. Herdman now?
- If Mrs. Armstrong hadn't fallen and broken her leg, would the Herdmans have been in the pageant?
- Why didn't Mrs. Herdman stay home and take care of her children?
- What would happen if Mr. Herdman came home?
- Did King Herod really die peacefully at home?
- Will Mrs. Armstrong be in charge of the pageant next year?
- Do you think that Mary was like Imogene?
- Was it truly the "best Christmas pageant ever"?
- Did Mrs. Herdman go to the pageant?
- Why was Imogene crying?
- What will the Herdmans do with the set of Bible story pictures?
- Why did the Herdmans give their ham to Baby Jesus?
- How did Alice Wendleken react to the pageant?
- Will the Herdmans behave differently now?
- Do the Herdmans volunteer to be in the pageant next year?
- Do Charlie and Leroy become friends?

Book Report Ideas

There are many ways to do a book report. After you have finished reading *The Best Christmas Pageant Ever*, choose one method of reporting that interests you. It may be a way that your teacher suggests, an idea of your own, or one of the ways below.

■ From the Artist

A model of a scene from the story can be created, or a likeness of one or more of the characters from the story can be drawn or sculpted.

■ Time Capsule

Make a time capsule-type design for future readers. Neatly print your reasons why *The Best Christmas Pageant Ever* is such a good book. Store your time capsule in the library for future readers.

■ Come to Life!

In a group, dress as characters from a scene in the book. Using props, act out that scene for the rest of the class.

■ Into the Future

This report predicts what might happen if *The Best Christmas Pageant Ever* were to continue. It may take the form of a story in narrative or dramatic form, or a visual display.

■ Twenty Questions

A reporter gives a series of clues about a character or an event in the story, in a vague-to-precise, general-to-specific order. After all clues have been given, the identity of the mystery character or event is guessed.

■ A Character Comes to Life!

Suppose one of the characters in *The Best Christmas Pageant Ever* came to life and walked into your home or school. Write about what the character sees, hears, and feels as he or she experiences the world in which you live.

■ Sales Talk

Dress as a salesperson. Write a sales pitch and design some kind of graphics in an effort to sell *The Best Christmas Pageant Ever* to your classmates.

■ Coming Attraction!

The Best Christmas Pageant Ever is about to be made into a movie, and you have been chosen to design the promotional poster. Include the title and author of the book, a listing of the main characters, and the contemporary actors who will play them. Illustrate a scene from the book, and write a brief synopsis of the story.

■ Literary Interview

This report is done in pairs. One student will pretend to be a character in the story and will be dressed as that character. The other student will play the role of a TV or radio interviewer, trying to provide the audience with insights into the character's life and personality.

Research Ideas

Describe three things that you read in *The Best Christmas Pageant Ever* that you would like to learn more about.

1. _____

2. _____

3. _____

To increase your understanding of the characters and events of the book, as well as appreciate Barbara Robinson's craft as a writer, research to find out more about the story's background.

Work in groups to research one or more of the areas you named above or the areas listed below. Share your findings with the rest of the class in any appropriate format for oral presentation.

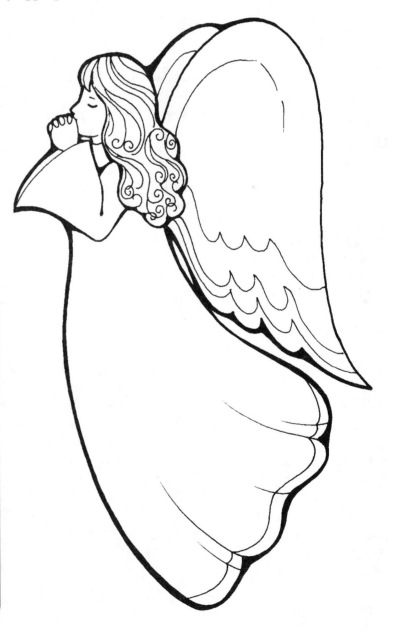

The Christmas Story
- ✤ Mary
- ✤ Joseph
- ✤ Jesus
- ✤ The Three Wise Men
- ✤ King Herod
- ✤ The Angel of the Lord

Bethlehem
- ✤ Today
- ✤ Yesterday
- ✤ The stable
- ✤ Can you visit the birthplace of Jesus today?

Christmas
- ✤ Around the world
- ✤ Customs
- ✤ Traditions
- ✤ Crafts
- ✤ Recipes
- ✤ Beliefs
- ✤ Stories

Now Playing: Reader's Theater!

Reader's Theater is a style of performance presented by players dressed as characters from a book. The players first select a passage from the book to reenact. Then they write a script, practice performing, choose costumes, and recreate the scene for their audience.

Materials:

- One large trunk filled with a collection of costumes
- One popcorn popper and popcorn
- Tickets to the theater

Directions:

1. Divide your students into teams of four or five players.
2. Have the teams choose a scene from *The Best Christmas Pageant Ever.* (A quick way to get started with this technique is to duplicate the desired passages directly from the book, and have the students highlight their parts).
3. Choose costumes from the theater trunk and practice, practice, practice!
4. When your team is ready to present, give each member of the audience a ticket to the performance. Have a "ticket taker" stand by the classroom door and collect the tickets as the audience enters. Assign someone the task of popcorn maker. Have him/her make popcorn and pass it out before the performance.

ADMIT ONE

to a performance of

The Best Christmas Pageant Ever

Possible Scenes:

- ★ Claude brings the Herdman cat to school. (Chapter 1)
- ★ Imogene tells Mother that she wants to be Mary. (Chapter 3)
- ★ The first pageant rehearsal. (Chapter 4)
- ★ Mrs. McCarthy calls the fire department. (Chapter 6)
- ★ The pageant. (Chapter 7)

Tips for Acting:

- ✔ Speak loudly and clearly.
- ✔ Practice your lines so that you can say them without a script.
- ✔ Use expression and emotion; pretend that you really are that character.
- ✔ Have fun!

Puppet Show Time!

Using the script you wrote on page 34, put on a puppet show for the younger children in your school. You may wish to invite them to your classroom, the library, or you may bring your program to their room.

As a whole group, brainstorm the order in which the chapters should be presented, the characters and how they will be introduced, and the main ideas that will be presented in your program. You must also decide who will be the puppeteers and the narrators. Directions for creating felt puppets are provided on the next page.

Make a Puppet Stage

If you have a ready-made puppet theater in your school you may wish to use it. However, you can create your own. Consider the following ideas:

Table: Hang an old sheet over a low table. The puppeteers simply kneel on the floor behind the table and move the puppets on the top of it.

Box: Cut a large, square hole in the top half of a big box, prop up the box, and have the puppeteers sit or kneel behind the box.

Sheet: Hang a rope or heavy string across a corner of the room about two feet (60 cm) from the floor. Drop a sheet over the rope. The puppeteers kneel behind the sheet in the corner and move the puppets above the sheet.

Establish Rules

Have a class discussion to decide the rules for puppet play. Include a discussion about being too rough with the puppets. Print the rules on a chart and display in your classroom.

Practice

You may wish to pre-record music as a background for your presentation. Then, PRACTICE before your performance so that things go as smoothly as possible. Good Luck!

Create Felt Puppets

For your puppet show, you'll need puppets. You can create puppets out of socks, paper bags, paper and sticks, or out of felt. To create felt puppets, gather the materials listed and follow the directions below. Create the number of puppets you'll need to perform your script.

Materials:

- Tan felt (one yard/ 91 cm is enough for 7 puppets)
- Scraps of colored felt
- Small black buttons (for eyes)
- Glue
- Yarn (for hair)
- Scissors

Directions:

1. Fold the tan felt in half, and pin the puppet pattern piece in place. Because you doubled the felt, you'll cut out two pieces, which you need for each puppet.

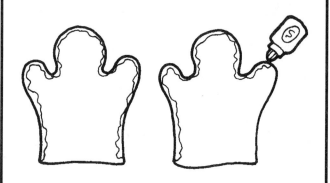

2. On the wrong side of each piece, draw a line of glue along the outer edge. Place the two pieces together and allow to dry.

3. Glue the black buttons on for eyes. Cut felt pieces for the mouth and nose; glue in place.

4. Cut the yarn in six-inch (15 cm) strips and glue in place for the hair. Decorate with the scraps of colored felt.

        ©1994 Teacher Created Materials, Inc.

Puppet Pattern

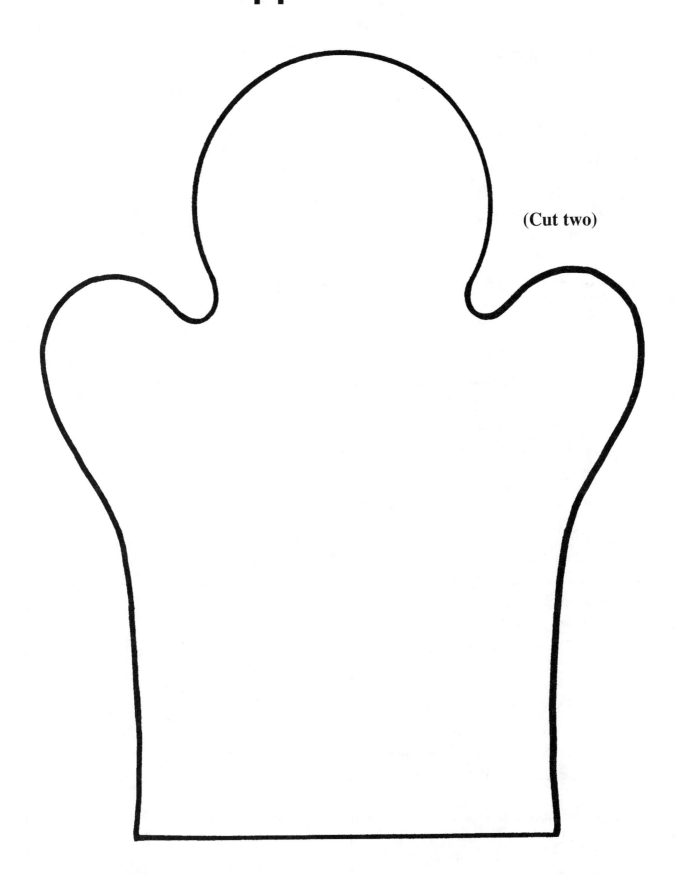

(Cut two)

Objective Test and Essay

Matching

Match the descriptions of the characters with their names.

1. _____ Imogene
2. _____ Mother
3. _____ Father
4. _____ Leroy
5. _____ Ollie
6. _____ Gladys
7. _____ Mrs. Armstrong
8. _____ Charlie
9. _____ Miss Graebner
10. _____ Alice Wendleken

A. Always taking notes on the Herdmans
B. The narrator's brother
C. Famous for pussy willows in his ear
D. The Angel of the Lord
E. Likes his dinner on time
F. A very bossy lady
G. The librarian
H. Always making Charlie black and blue
I. She gives the Herdmans a chance.
J. She blackmails her classmates and steals money from the collection basket.

True or False

Answer true or false in the blanks below.

1. _____ King Herod died of old age.
2. _____ Imogene finally realized the beauty of Christmas.
3. _____ Mrs. Armstrong broke her leg.
4. _____ The Herdmans came to church for the refreshments.
5. _____ Alice Wendleken wore Vaseline® on her eyelids.

Short Answer

Write a brief response to each question in the space provided.

1. Where did the Herdmans get the ham that they gave as a gift during the pageant?
2. Why was it the best Christmas pageant ever?
3. How did Imogene get her black eye?
4. What did the Herdmans take as a gift after the pageant?
5. Why do you think Imogene was crying?

Essay

Write an essay on the topics below. Use your own paper.

1. Why do you think the Herdmans wouldn't take any candy or Bibles?
2. What do you think Imogene meant when she said that the picture of Mary was "exactly right"?
3. The townspeople didn't like the Herdmans, at first. What did they learn from the Herdmans?

Essay Challenge: Include in your essay what you think the Herdmans were like after the pageant.

Response

Explain the meaning of these quotations from *The Best Christmas Pageant Ever.*

Note to the Teacher: Choose the appropriate number of quotes to which your students should respond.

Chapter 1:   *The Herdmans were absolutely the worst kids in the history of the world.*

Chapter 1:   *One day Claude Herdman emptied the whole first grade in three minutes flat when he took the cat to Show-and-Tell.*

Chapter 1:   *As far as anyone could tell, Imogene was just like the rest of the Herdmans. She never learned anything either, except dirty words and secrets about everybody.*

Chapter 1:   *Actually, they didn't know what their father was or where he was or anything about him, because when Gladys was two years old he climbed on a railroad train and disappeared. Nobody blamed him.*

Chapter 2:   *My little brother, Charlie stood up and he didn't even have to look at his piece of paper. "What I like best about Sunday school," he said, "is that there aren't any Herdmans here."*

Chapter 2:   *In the end it was Charlie's fault that the Herdmans showed up in church.*

Chapter 3:   *Actually there was somebody at the door. It was my father, standing out on the porch in his coat and hat, leaning on the doorbell.*

Chapter 3:   *But I knew—I'd heard Imogene Herdman telling Alice what would happen to her if she dared to volunteer: all the ordinary, everyday Herdman-things like clonking you on the head, and drawing pictures all over your homework papers, and putting worms in your coat pocket.*

Chapter 3:   *He just reminded everyone that when Jesus said, "Suffer the little children to come unto me," Jesus meant all the children, including Herdmans.*

Chapter 4:   *I couldn't understand the Herdmans. You would have thought the Christmas story came right out of the F.B.I. files, they got so involved in it—wanted a bloody end to Herod, worried about Mary having her baby in a barn, and called the Wise Men a bunch of dirty spies.*

Chapter 5:   *One day I saw Alice Wendleken writing something down on a little pad of paper, and trying to hide it with her other hand.*

Chapter 5:   *But when all the mothers found out about the Herdmans they withdrew their babies.*

Chapter 6:   *Mother was wrong—everybody in that end of town knew we were there before the evening was over.*

Chapter 6:   *Well, we never did go right straight through. The five-minute recess was a big mistake, because it stretched to fifteen minutes, and Imogene spent the whole time smoking cigars in one of the johns in the ladies' room.*

Chapter 7:   *When it was over people stood around the lobby of the church talking about what was different this year. There was something special, everyone said—they couldn't put their finger on what.*

Conversations

Work in size-appropriate groups to write and perform the conversation that might have occurred in one of the following situations. If you prefer, you may use your own conversation idea for characters from *The Best Christmas Pageant Ever.*

- ✠ Leroy and Imogene discussing the fire the night they burned down Mr. Shoemaker's toolhouse. (2 people)

- ✠ Claude and Miss Brandel the day he emptied the classroom with his cat during Show-and-Tell. (2 people)

- ✠ Imogene explaining to the younger Herdmans about where their father was and when he'd be home. (4 people)

- ✠ Miss Phillips and Mrs. Herdman discussing her staying home more with her children. (2 people)

- ✠ Mrs. Armstrong and Mother discussing the pageant and the Herdmans. (2 people)

- ✠ The Herdmans talking about their first day in church. (6 people)

- ✠ Alice Wendleken reporting to her mother about the Herdmans' behavior. (2 people)

- ✠ Imogene threatening the other children if they dared to volunteer for any of the parts in the pageant. (8 or more people)

- ✠ The nurse and Ollie the day she discovered the pussy willow growing in his ear. (2 people)

- ✠ The Herdmans in the library discussing the Christmas story. (6 people)

- ✠ Mother and Father discussing the night that the fire department was called during rehearsal. (2 people)

- ✠ Mrs. Wendleken's phone call to Reverend Hopkins after the "fire." (2 people)

- ✠ The Herdmans deciding to give their Christmas ham to Baby Jesus. (6 people)

- ✠ Reverend Hopkins and Mrs. Wendleken talking after the pageant. (2 people)

- ✠ Mother, the following year, when she is asked to do the pageant again. (2 people)

Bibliography of Related

Brett, Jan. *The Wild Christmas Reindeer.* Putnam, 1990.

Bunting, Eve. *Night Tree.* Harcourt Brace Jovanovich, 1991.

Cuyler, Margery. *The All-Around Christmas Book.* Holt, 1982.

DePaola, Tomie. *The Family Christmas Tree Book.* Holiday House, 1980.

DePaola, Tomie. *The Legend of Old Befana.* Harcourt, 1980.

Dickens, Charles. *A Christmas Carol.* Random House, 1990.

Greenberg, Martin H. and Charles G. Waugh. *A Newberry Christmas.* Delacorte, 1991.

Haywood, Carolyn. *How the Reindeer Saved Christmas.* Morrow, 1986.

Moore, Clement C. *The Night Before Christmas.* Gareth Stevens Publisher, 1985.

Naylor, Phyllis Reynolds. *Old Sadie and the Christmas Bear.* Atheneum, 1984.

Purdy, Susan. *Christmas Cookbook.* Watts, 1976.

Rosen, Michael. *Elijah's Angel.* Harcourt Brace Jovanovich, 1992.

Rylant, Cynthia. *Children of Christmas, Stories for the Season.* Orchard Books, 1987.

Tudor, Tasha. *Take Joy! The Tasha Tudor Christmas Book.* World Publisher, 1966.

Van Allsburg, Chris. *The Polar Express.* Houghton-Mifflin, 1985.

Watts, Bernadette. *The Fir Tree.* North-South Books, 1990.

Yolen, Jane. *Hark! A Christmas Sampler.* Putnam, 1991.

Teacher Resources

Black, Naomi. *The Whole Christmas Catalogue.* Tern Enterprises, 1986.

Linsley, Leslie. *Christmas Ornaments and Stockings.* St. Martin's Press, 1982.

Low, Alice. *The Family Read-Aloud Christmas Treasury.* Little Brown and Company, 1989.

Meras, Phyllis and Juliana Turkevich. *Christmas Angels.* Houghton Mifflin, 1979.

Stewart, Shelley and Jo Voce. *Decorating and Craft Ideas for Christmas.* Oxmoor House, 1984.

Answer Key

Page 10

1. Accept appropriate answers.
2. They were using Leroy's chemistry set, and they started a fire.
3. The Herdmans took them.
4. Accept appropriate answers.
5. The cat was mad and wild. It flew out of the box and scratched its way down the blackboard, landing on the chalkboard rail. Then it began to scratch at everything in sight, including the children, desks, papers, and the teacher. Miss Brandel covered her head with her coat and tried to coax the cat into the corner. She screamed for Claude to help her, but he didn't.
6. She blackmailed them by finding out how much they weighed and she threatened to tell everyone if they didn't give her what she wanted.
7. No one really knows. He simply left one day and never came back.
8. They take care of each other.
9. Barbara Robinson; 1972.
10. They were too horrible.

Page 15

1. It is a play about the birth of Jesus.
2. A shepherd.
3. To make her children be in it and to make her husband go to it.
4. Mrs. Armstrong.
5. Mrs. Armstrong broke her leg.
6. The Herdmans aren't there.
7. Leroy.
8. He told Leroy that they served refreshments.
9. For the refreshments.
10. She stole money from it.

Page 20

1. Mrs. Armstrong.
2. Mary.
3. Father.
4. She never had dinner ready when he got home.
5. Imogene.
6. Joseph.
7. Ralph.
8. Imogene threatened them.
9. A pussy willow.
10. They were very upset.

Page 26

1. Sly and sneaky.
2. Drew tails and mustaches on the disciples.
3. In a dresser drawer.
4. They were fascinated.
5. They didn't like him.

6. The library.
7. He was the king who demanded Jesus' death.
8. To tell her mother so that she could be Mary.
9. They heard that the Herdmans were in the play.
10. A doll.

Page 31

1. Ladies from the church.
2. Vaseline.
3. Gladys.
4. Smoking cigars.
5. Mrs. McCarthy thought the ladies room was on fire.
6. It burned.
7. They were poor and people didn't care about them.
8. The ham.
9. They brought their own innocence and sense of wonder to it.
10. She realized the true meaning of Christmas.

Page 44

Matching
1. J
2. I
3. E
4. H
5. C
6. D
7. F
8. B
9. G
10. A

True or False
1. True
2. True
3. True
4. True
5. True

Short Answer
1. Their Christmas basket.
2. The Herdmans made it real.
3. She ran into the corner of the cabinet.
4. Bible-story pictures.
5. She was touched by the meaning of Christmas.

Essay

Answers will vary. Accept all reasonable and well supported answers.

Page 45

Accept all well supported responses.

Page 46

Perform the conversations in class.